TO BIGOTRY NO SANCTION
GEORGE WASHINGTON AND RELIGIOUS FREEDOM

NATIONAL MUSEUM OF
AMERICAN JEWISH HISTORY

National Museum of American Jewish History
101 South Independence Mall East
Philadelphia, Pennsylvania 19106-2517
www.nmajh.org

This book has been published in conjunction with the special exhibition
To Bigotry No Sanction: George Washington and Religious Freedom
June 29 - September 30, 2012
by the National Museum of American Jewish History

Catalogue Design by Courtney Ballantine

Copyright 2012 by the National Museum of American Jewish History

ISBN: 978-1-891507-02-1

Printed in the United States of America

Cover Image:
Detail, Letter from George Washington to the Hebrew Congregation in Newport, 1790
Courtesy of the Morris Morgenstern Foundation

Contents

Introduction

Arguably the single most important document in American Jewish history, George Washington's 1790 letter to the Newport Jewish community represents a courageous and historic statement by America's first national leader, one which affirmed both rights and privileges generally unknown to Jews for millennia and, even more importantly, underscored the new nation's commitment to religious liberty and equality for people of all faiths. I could not be more proud that the National Museum of American Jewish History is the first venue in more than a decade to share with a wide public this remarkable piece of American and American Jewish history.

With immense gratitude to the Morris Morgenstern Foundation, we are thrilled to display this letter as the centerpiece of *To Bigotry No Sanction: George Washington and Religious Freedom*—the first special exhibition in our new home, appropriately opening in time for the Fourth of July. The stunning constellation of historically significant objects that we have gathered for this exhibition recounts, animates, and gives insight into the remarkable period in which religious freedom was established in America and allows visitors to track the unfolding of this national conversation.

Presented now, in a presidential election year when Americans and their leaders are again engaging in passionate debates about faith, identity, and politics, this groundbreaking exhibition stands as a powerful reminder of the ideals and freedoms that lie at the core of this nation.

As the only museum in the nation dedicated solely to telling the American Jewish story from 1654 to the present, in a core exhibition that interprets how Jews shape and are shaped by

View of *Religious Liberty* by Moses Ezekiel, outside the National Museum of American Jewish History
Copyright Jeff Goldberg/Esto

America, and explores the blessings and challenges of freedom—there could be no more perfect venue for this exhibition. When I consider that many of the documents featured in this special exhibition were conceived or penned in our very neighborhood over two hundred years ago, I feel deeply honored to exhibit them here, on Independence Mall, in the heart of historic Philadelphia, at the site of America's birth.

A project of this significance came together in no small part due to the support and generosity of our Board of Trustees, whose commitment to providing opportunities for people of all faiths and backgrounds to make the Museum their own allows us to present exhibitions that explore freedom for all Americans through the lens of the American Jewish story. In record time and with customary passion and professionalism, our chief curator Josh Perelman and his staff brought together a collection of exceptional artifacts with which to round out this story. As always, our chief historian Jonathan D. Sarna provided invaluable insight to ensure that our exhibition most deftly interprets the Washington correspondence and its historical significance. I am also grateful to Facing History and Ourselves for allowing us to include here, in the exhibition, and on the Web, Dr. Sarna's annotations on the Seixas and Washington letters. In addition, Seth Kaller provided vital assistance as both a lender and consultant on this project.

A number of private individuals and public institutions have graciously loaned one-of-a-kind artifacts to the Museum for this special occasion and turned around our loan requests with unheard-of alacrity: Boston Public Library Rare Books Department, Congregation Mikveh Israel in Philadelphia, Haverford College Quaker and Special Collections, Seth Kaller, Deanne and Arnold Kaplan, the Morris Morgenstern Foundation, Mount Vernon Ladies' Association, National Archives, Philadelphia Museum of Art, David Rubenstein, and Yeshiva University Museum, as well as an anonymous lender.

When I came to the Museum one year ago, I knew that we were poised to take our place on the Mall as a preeminent national museum that creatively teaches, interprets, and inspires dialogue about the American Jewish experience in the context of American history and fuels the spirit of courage and imagination, aspiration and leadership, that characterizes the founding leaders of our country as well as our very own ancestors. Richard Morgenstern's confidence in the Museum's vision and ability, and the extraordinary conviction and leadership our Board of

Trustees, have helped realize the dream of interpreting faith and freedom in early America. It is my sincere hope that the outstanding artifacts brought together for *To Bigotry No Sanction: George Washington and Religious Freedom* enable us to broaden our reach as an institution and to be a destination for showcasing historic treasures that are profoundly relevant and resonant to Philadelphians, to its visitors from all over the world, and to all Americans.

Ivy L. Barsky
Gwen Goodman Director and CEO
Philadelphia, June 2012

It would be inconsistent with the frankness of my character not to avow that I am pleased with your favorable opinion of my administration, and fervent wishes for my felicity. May the children of the Stock of Abraham, who dwell in this land, continue to merit and enjoy the good will of the other Inhabitants; while every one shall sit in safety under his own vine and figtree, and there shall be none to make him afraid. May the father of all mercies scatter light and not darkness in our paths, and make us all in our several vocations useful here, and in his own due time and way everlastingly happy.

G: Washington

Preface

In August 1790, Moses Seixas, sexton of the Hebrew Congregation of Newport, Rhode Island, penned an articulate and beautiful welcome to President George Washington upon his reception at the synagogue, praising the Almighty for victory in the recent War of Independence and for saving Mr. Washington from harm. In his missive Seixas actually wrote the immortal words and oft-repeated mantra "to bigotry no sanction, to persecution no assistance" as well as other language that the president wove into his rejoinder.

George Washington's iconic response—easily his most significant writing, a major piece of American history, and a cornerstone of expression of the American ideal—is as timeless, powerful, and eloquent today as ever: that there are inherent natural rights to worship in freedom and, by inference, to express one's global individualism, unafraid. Like a wonderful dream, the letter depicts a paradigm of endless possibility afforded to our new nation, populated by people of goodwill.

The Morris Morgenstern Foundation is thrilled to join with the National Museum of American Jewish History in bringing these documents to the public. The world could do worse than to heed the enduring wisdom embodied in George Washington's words.

Richard P. Morgenstern,
for the Morris Morgenstern Foundation

A Revolutionary Promise

Dr. Josh Perelman

Chief Curator and Director of Exhibitions and Collections, National Museum of American Jewish History

"Every one shall sit in safety under his own vine and fig-tree, and there shall be none to make him afraid."
-George Washington to the Hebrew Congregation in Newport, 1790

George Washington made his first presidential visit to Newport, Rhode Island, on August 17, 1790, traveling there only after the state had become the last to ratify the Constitution. Rhode Island welcomed the president with laudatory addresses from representatives of government as well as civic and religious institutions, including Newport's Congregation Yeshuat Israel.[1] Moses Seixas, speaking on behalf of the congregation, celebrated that the new Constitution offered Jews "the invaluable rights of free citizens," privileges denied them in most other countries.[2] Upon returning to New York City, Washington composed a letter of thanks to the Jewish community that had welcomed him, one whose 340 words stand as the most moving and courageous affirmation of religious liberty ever to be penned by an American president.

Fourteen years had passed since the signing of the Declaration of Independence, and Washington, the revered hero, had been president for just over a year. His letter to the "Hebrew Congregation in Newport" stated unequivocally that Americans had the right "to applaud themselves for having given mankind examples of an enlarged and liberal policy: a policy worthy of imitation." Washington wrote that, unlike in Europe, in this American nation "it is now no more that toleration is spoken of, as if it was by the indulgence of one class of people, that another enjoyed the exercise of their inherent natural rights." He followed this statement with a revolutionary promise: echoing Seixas's address, Washington "happily" asserted that the new nation would give "to bigotry no sanction, to persecution no assistance." This right to participate fully in a democracy had never before been guaranteed to Jews in the modern era.

George Washington
Gilbert Charles Stuart, 1796
National Portrait Gallery, Smithsonian Institution; acquired as a gift to the nation
through the generosity of the Donald W. Reynolds Foundation

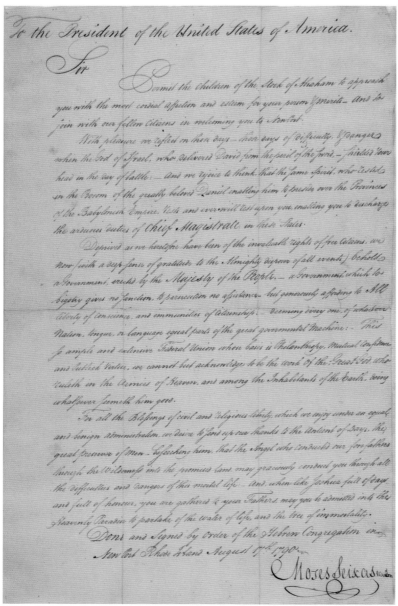

Letter to George Washington, Signed by Moses Seixas, 1790
Courtesy of the Morris Morgenstern Foundation

The exchange between the first American president and the Jewish community of Newport is the centerpiece for the National Museum of American Jewish History's inaugural special exhibition, *To Bigotry No Sanction: George Washington and Religious Freedom.* Framing Washington's letter is a selection of iconic documents, publications, and portraits from both American and American Jewish history, including important editions of this nation's foundational documents—the Declaration of Independence, the Constitution, and the Bill of Rights—and letters illustrating George Washington's statements about religious freedom to America's Jewish and Christian communities during his first two years in office. These artifacts underscore how George Washington's correspondence with Newport's Jews serves as a remarkable expression of the era when religious freedom was being established in the new nation. Moreover, as a group, they point to the significance of the historic city in which this exhibition is presented: Philadelphia. The drama of forming a new nation took place here, on and around Independence Mall, and many of early America's most prominent citizens, Jewish and Christian, called it home.[3]

Today Americans often take it for granted that we live in a country where people of all faiths enjoy the freedom to believe and worship as we please. Although we by no means agree on matters of religion, our debates occur in an environment where no single belief system or denomination can claim authority based on a mandate from the federal government. At the time of our nation's founding, however, religious communities could not assume that this would be true. People intently followed the debate about the nature and limits of the new American government and its approach to religion, seeking assurance that their rights would be protected.[4] They were not disappointed.

Still, the policies and promises made by America's founding documents and political leaders, however majestic, came with a host of complexities and imperfections: the freedoms they offered were revolutionary but could not be enjoyed by all living in America. For instance, Washington's May 1789 letter to the Methodist Episcopal church, with its pledge to ensure the "preservation of the civil and religious liberties of the American people," arrived at a moment of growing racial tensions in Philadelphia's Methodist community— where for decades whites and free blacks had worshiped together— that resulted in the departure of its African American congregants in protest. This, despite the fact that several years earlier Methodist leaders had visited the future president at Mount Vernon to solicit his signature on a petition to the Virginia Assembly "for the immediate or Gradual Extirpation of Slavery."[5] Even as we continue to wrestle with the legacy of these flaws, they do not diminish the significance of what our founding documents achieved; nor should these flaws overshadow the critical importance or the impact of Washington's leadership. His determination to ensure that the nation lived up to its offer of religious freedom is as meaningful today as it must have been at the time of his presidency.

"Back of the State House, Philadelphia"
William Russell Birch, *The City of Philadelphia, in the State of Pennsylvania North America*, 1799
Print and Picture Collection, Free Library of Philadelphia

An East Prospect of the City of Philadelphia
Thomas Jefferys, 1754
The New York Public Library

Thomas Jefferson
Mather Brown, 1786
National Portrait Gallery, Smithsonian Institution; bequest of Charles Francis Adams

which asserted that "the natural rights of mankind" included the freedom "to profess, and by argument to maintain, their opinions in matters of religion." Introduced in 1779, the act passed with slight modifications in 1786. Four years later, Jefferson served as secretary of state and accompanied Washington to Newport, making it possible that the two exchanged ideas about the composition of Washington's letter.

On the heels of independence came a dramatic decade and a half during which "Americans had been designing and redesigning their governments."[7] Washington understood that as a consequence of the Articles of Confederation's failure to provide a stable framework for government "the situation amounted to a crisis of unprecedented importance for the young nation." America's most prominent citizen set out for Philadelphia on May 8, 1787, to attend the federal convention.[8]

The convention had met behind closed doors, and no Jew is known to have attended. Nor is there a documented instance of Jews being discussed during the proceedings. Nevertheless, in early September 1787, a German Jewish merchant from Philadelphia, Jonas Phillips, sent a letter "To those in whom there is wisdom understanding and knowledge . . . the honourable personages appointed and Made overseers of a part of the terrestrial globe of the Earth, Namely the 13 united states of america in Convention Assembled, the Lord preserve them amen." Phillips knew that Pennsylvania's 1776 state constitution required elected officials to swear faith in the Christian scripture, a religious test that prevented Jews from holding office. "The Israelites will think themself happy," he wrote, "to live under a government where all Religious societys are on an Equal footing."[9] Although it is unknown whether delegates read Phillips's plea for equality or if it had an impact on their deliberations, protests like this did lead Pennsylvania to change its policies when it issued a new state constitution in 1790.[10]

The earliest known publication of the Declaration of Independence in Massachusetts, known as the "Salem Broadside," hinted at the new nation's approach to religion by proclaiming that "all men are created equal, that they are endowed by their Creator with certain unalienable rights." Furthermore, it pointed to the crucial role that its author, Thomas Jefferson, played in defining American freedom, as both a political leader and a close friend to George Washington.[6] Shortly after authoring the Declaration, Jefferson drafted the Virginia Act for Establishing Religious Freedom,

Four months later, on September 17, 1787, publishers John Dunlap and David Claypoole issued the first public printing of the United States Constitution in their newspaper, *The Pennsylvania Packet*. The Constitution included no discussion of Jews and spent very little time addressing religion.[11]

From the perspective of religious minorities like Jews, the Constitution's framework for "a more perfect Union" took a crucial step toward religious freedom by banning religious tests for public office. Article VI, Section 2, affirmed that all elected officials "shall be bound by Oath or Affirmation, to support this Constitution; but no religious Test shall ever be required as a Qualification to any Office or public Trust under the United States." Soon thereafter Congress took up the issue of religion in the twelve amendments it proposed to the Constitution in 1789. As the "Ratification of the Bill of Rights by the Commonwealth of Pennsylvania" illustrates, what we now recognize as the First Amendment, establishing freedom of religion, speech, press, and peaceful assembly, was originally listed third. Indeed, Pennsylvania ratified only ten of the amendments, rejecting the first and second, regarding ratio of representation and congressional pay, respectively.

By making matters of faith an individual or communal concern, rather than a governmental mandate, the framers clearly distinguished the new nation from its European peers.[12] American Jews achieved religious rights "as individuals along with everybody else," according to historian Jonathan Sarna, "not, as so often the case in Europe and the Caribbean, through a special privilege or 'Jew Bill' that set them apart as a group."[13] During the same period western and central European countries were taking steps toward emancipation, but the offering of limited rights was predicated upon the belief that greater social integration would lead Jews to convert, and in any case, these rights could always be taken away at the whim of a particular ruler. In Russia no

Constitutional Convention
Junius Brutus Stearns
The Granger Collection, New York

such tenuous bargains existed. The 1791 confinement of Jews to a specific geographic area called the Pale of Settlement, along with periodic episodes of violence, increasingly constrained Jews' economic and political rights and often endangered their lives.[14]

The Constitution and Bill of Rights provided the foundation for American religious liberty, transforming the lives of Jews and more broadly the role of religion in the United States. It became policy that the federal government would have no official say in matters of religious practice. All Americans would be free to choose how and where to exercise religion and which beliefs (or nonbelief, if that suited) would sustain their spiritual lives. For the nearly 2,500 Jews who lived in America, this opened the door to an unprecedented sense of integration. Yet, the same documents that expressed America's best ideals and granted citizenship to all white men offered no political rights to women and lawfully perpetuated slavery.

Mordecai Manuel Noah
John Wesley Jarvis, ca. 1820
The Jacob Rader Marcus Center of the American Jewish Archives

America also did not live up to its promises of religious freedom in all circumstances. The Constitution only applied to the actions of the federal government and did not restrict states from discriminating on the basis of religion. So, while many states eliminated religious oaths for holding office, Jews did not win full rights in every state until 1877. Moreover, even though American Jews achieved social and economic integration far and beyond that of most European Jews, antisemitism would continue to be a characteristic of American life during and after the revolutionary era.[15] This is evident in the career of Mordecai Manuel Noah, grandson of Jonas Phillips and America's most

prominent Jew in the early nineteenth century. A journalist, playwright, judge, and politician, Noah accepted diplomatic appointments to Latvia in 1811 and Tunis in 1813, earning him the highest position achieved by a Jew at the time. Yet, when secretary of state James Monroe recalled Noah from Tunis in 1815, he cited religion as the motivating factor for the change. Three years later, Noah sent Thomas Jefferson a transcript of the address he gave when New York's Congregation Shearith Israel consecrated its new synagogue building. Noah noted the continued intolerance toward Jews abroad and described America as the Jews' "chosen country." Jefferson, in his response, acknowledged that "more remains to be done, for altho' we are free by the law, we are not so in practice."[16]

Despite the prejudices of many of his peers, George Washington remained a steadfast champion of religious freedom. He assured the United Baptists of Virginia in a 1789 letter: "If I could have entertained the slightest apprehension that the Constitution framed in the Convention, where I had the honor to preside, might possibly endanger the religious rights of any ecclesiastical society, certainly I would never have placed my signature to it."[17] When Washington became president on April 30, 1789, Americans showered their new leader with festivities, parades, and joyful addresses. Jews expressed their support for America's ideals in special prayers and synagogue constitutions. Included in this exhibition is the Hebrew prayer composed by Jacob I. Cohen of Richmond's Congregation Beth Shalome, North America's sixth synagogue, for November 26, 1789, the first "Day of Publick Thanksgiving and Prayer." Washington had proclaimed that day as a time for the nation to thank "that great and glorious Being" for "the peaceable and rational manner in which we have been enabled to establish Constitutions of government for our safety and happiness." Cohen's composition, known as "The Richmond Prayer," offered heartfelt words of praise for the new nation and its leaders and spelled out the name "Washington" in bold as a Hebrew acrostic along its right-hand margin.[18]

Jews celebrated Washington's inauguration and, along with other religious communities, hoped he would build upon the Constitution's elimination of a religious test to serve in any governmental office. America's first president, boldly confirming the new nation's commitment to religious freedom, did not let them down. Savannah's Jews applauded Washington for having "dispelled that cloud of bigotry and superstition which has long, as a veil, shaded religion." The Jews of Philadelphia, New York, Charleston, and Richmond wrote to Washington as a group and thanked him for opening "the way to the reign of freedom." Christian denominations across the religious spectrum also wrote to praise the new president and ensure their rights. In all, Washington wrote eighteen letters to American religious communities, emphasizing to each that religious liberty "is not only among the choicest of their blessings, but also of their rights."[19]

Yet it is Washington's remarkable exchange with the "Hebrew Congregation in Newport" and his iconic promise of a government that "gives to bigotry no sanction, to persecution no assistance" that have stood the test of time and remind us of the continuing role we play in ensuring their preservation. Reprinted, republished, and continuously revisited since the time of its writing, Washington's letter captures the moment in American history when democracy and pluralism were being established as the defining principles of a new nation. Most importantly, its message continues to be as relevant today as it was 222 years ago, a timeless reminder of the ideals that lie at this nation's heart. "If we have wisdom to make the best use of the advantages with which we are now favored," America's first president wrote, "we cannot fail, under the just administration of a good Government, to become a great and a happy people."

To Bigotry No Sanction has benefited from the enthusiasm, generosity, and creativity of an extraordinary community of lenders, advisors, designers, and colleagues: I am indebted to their counsel and to the inspiration they have given me. An institution-wide dedication to this exhibition and the immeasurable support of the Board of Trustees and Ivy Barsky, the Museum's Gwen Goodman Director and CEO, provided the essential backing required for an undertaking of this significance. This, paired with the exuberance, professionalism, and thoughtfulness of my colleagues in the exhibitions and collections department and the investment by the entire Museum staff, made planning for this exhibition an immense pleasure. It has been a privilege to witness how 340 words and the events and ideas they represent have stirred their imaginations and passions.

Inauguration of George Washington
Montbaron and Gautschi
Collection of The New-York Historical Society

Endnotes

1 Newport Congregation Yeshuat Israel (Salvation of Israel) dedicated its synagogue in 1763. Designed by prominent architect Peter Harrison, the dignified building blends in neatly with its neighborhood. Today known as the Touro Synagogue, it is the oldest surviving synagogue building in the United States.

2 Moses Seixas to President George Washington, August 17, 1790. Notably, Seixas also addressed Washington on behalf of the Masons, a marker of his prominence in the community. Maud Lyman Stevens, "Washington and Newport," *Bulletin of the Newport Historical Society 84* (1932). Any unattributed quotes in this essay are from this letter or Washington's response and a full transcript is included later in the catalogue.

3 Maxwell Whiteman and Edwin Wolf 2nd, *The History of the Jews of Philadelphia from Colonial Times to the Age of Jackson* (Philadelphia: Jewish Publication Society of America, 1975).

4 William Pencak, *Jews and Gentiles in Early America* (Ann Arbor: University of Michigan Press, 2005); Eli Faber, *A Time for Planting: The First Migration* (Baltimore: Johns Hopkins University Press, 1992).

5 John Wigger, *An American Saint: Francis Asbury and the Methodists.* (New York: Oxford University Press, 2009), 151-52, 246-48. A transcript of George Washington's letter to the Methodist Episcopal Church, May 29, 1789, is printed later in this catalogue.

6 Christopher Hitchens, *Thomas Jefferson: Author of America* (New York: HarperCollins, 2005).

7 Pauline Maier, *Ratification: The People Debate the Constitution* (New York: Simon & Schuster, 2010), 17; Gordon S. Wood, *The Creation of the American Republic, 1776–1787* (Chapel Hill: University of North Carolina Press, 1969), 356–67.

8 Notably, Rhode Island did not send delegates to the federal convention and refused to ratify the Constitution until 1790 for fear that the new government would impinge on its economic rights. On Rhode Island's refusal, see Maier, *Ratification*, 458–59.

9 Jonas Phillips to the federal convention, September 7, 1787. A transcript of this letter is printed later in this catalogue.

10 *The constitution of the commonwealth of Pennsylvania, as established by the general convention elected for that purpose & held at Philadelphia, July 15, 1776* (Philadelphia: Dunlap, 1777). In these instances of public advocacy, Jews often "walked a fine line between feeling part of the polity and entitled to full access and knowing that their Jewishness placed them in an outside category." Hasia R. Diner, *The Jews of the United States* (Berkeley: University of California Press, 2004), 37; Jonathan D. Sarna, *American Judaism* (New Haven, CT: Yale University Press, 2004), 60. Also see Beth S. Wenger, *The Jewish Americans: Three Centuries of Jewish Voices in America* (New York: Doubleday, 2007), 24–27, 39–43.

11 Diner, *Jews of the United States*, 48–56; Sarna, *American Judaism*, 36–41.

12 Diner, *Jews of the United States*, 2; Sarna, *American Judaism*, 55, 159.

13 Sarna, *American Judaism*, 37–38.

14 David B. Ruderman, *Early Modern Jewry: A New Cultural History* (Princeton, NJ: Princeton University Press, 2010).

15 After the Revolution, critics accused Haym Salomon, a broker for the Office of Finance, of supporting the war for personal, rather than patriotic, gain. In 1784, Salomon responded to an antisemitic attack from a congressman: "I am a Jew . . . I exult and glory in reflecting that we have the honour to reside in a free country." Similarly, Benjamin Nones, a Jewish veteran of the Revolutionary War, supported Thomas Jefferson in the 1800 presidential election. When Jefferson's opponents printed an antisemitic attack on Nones, he responded in the Philadelphia Aurora, "I am a Jew. I glory in belonging to that persuasion . . . I am a Republican! . . . I have not been so proud or so prejudiced as to renounce the cause for which I have fought, as an American throughout the whole of the revolutionary war . . . In republics we have rights, in monarchies we live but to experience wrongs . . . How then can a Jew but be a Republican?"

16 Thomas Jefferson to Mordecai Manuel Noah, May 28, 1818. A transcript of this letter is printed later in this catalogue.

17 George Washington to the United Baptists of Virginia, May 1789. A transcript of this letter is printed later in this catalogue.

18 A transcript of the "Richmond Prayer" is printed later in this catalogue. Other examples include "A Religious Discourse," a sermon delivered by Gershom Mendes Seixas at Congregation Shearith Israel in New York City on that same day, and Shearith Israel's constitution, composed in 1790.

19 George Washington to the Society of Quakers, October 1789. A transcript of this letter is printed later in this catalogue.

Detail, *Portrait of George Washington (The Dunn-Robinson Portrait of Washington)*
Gilbert Charles Stuart, ca. 1800
Philadelphia Museum of Art
Gift of the Honorable Walter H. Annenberg and Leonore Annenberg and the Annenberg Foundation, 2007

George Washington's Correspondence with the Jews of Newport

Dr. Jonathan D. Sarna

Chief Historian, National Museum of American Jewish History
Joseph H. and Belle R. Braun Professor of American Jewish History at Brandeis University

George Washington was inaugurated as president of the United States of America on April 30, 1789. The federal Constitution, by then, had been ratified by the requisite nine states and was in effect. Two other states soon signed on, and a twelfth state, North Carolina, ratified the Constitution in November 1789. Only Rhode Island, fearful that as a small state its rights would be trampled upon by the others, held back. It refused to ratify the Constitution, although it was already bound by it.

The new Constitution did not contain any clause guaranteeing religious liberty; that would only appear in the Bill of Rights in 1791. Article Six of the Constitution did outlaw religious tests "as a qualification to any office or public trust under the United States." That, for Jews and other non-Christians, marked a huge step forward as it guaranteed them the right to hold public offices in the federal government. The United States, unlike most countries with Christian majorities, promised non-Christians that they could, at least in theory, hold the highest governmental office in the land.

Washington wanted the new Constitution to be unanimously approved. He believed that would make all Americans feel a part of the great experiment that the United States represented; it would signify consensus. When Rhode Island held out against ratification, Washington publicly demonstrated his unhappiness by refusing to visit the state when he toured New England in the autumn of 1789. Only after Rhode Island finally ratified the Constitution on May 29, 1790, did he agree to travel there.

Three days after Congress adjourned, on August 15, he and a large entourage, including Secretary of State Thomas Jefferson, set out for Newport.

On August 18 four addresses (written, in keeping with the literary style of the day, in the form of open letters) were read out to the president at a prearranged ceremony; it was customary to greet visiting dignitaries in this way. There was an address from the town, a joint statement of welcome from all of the Christian clergy, and a greeting from the Masonic order (whose president was also the warden of the city's synagogue, Moses Seixas). The final and most historically important address came from the "Hebrew Congregation" – the community's Jews.

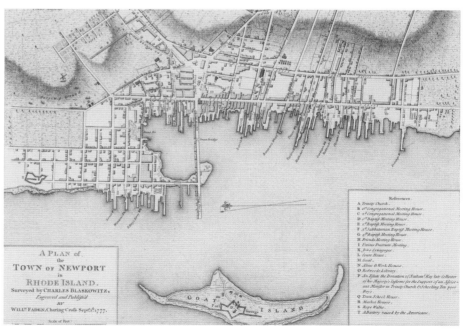

Map of Newport, 1777
Newport Historical Society

The fact that Jews were included at all is noteworthy. They formed a small but significant merchant community in Newport, and had built a beautiful synagogue, Yeshuat Israel, now known as the Touro Synagogue, in 1763. So, at the very end of Washington's visit to Newport, their representative stepped up to read an address to him. This was not the first Jewish address to Washington. That had come from the Jews of Savannah months earlier. And it was also not the last Jewish communication he received that year. Jews of New York, Philadelphia, Charleston, and Richmond sent him a joint letter several months later. But the Newport letter was, by general consensus, the most important of the lot, partly because of its content, and mostly because of his celebrated reply, sent a few days later from New York City.

Both letters were carefully written documents that reward close reading and minute study. To facilitate this, the letters are reprinted here; a commentary appears beside the text.

George Washington's correspondence with the Hebrew Congregation in Newport was published in newspapers across the country in 1790 and was frequently reprinted thereafter. A search on Google Books yields thousands of volumes that quote or reprint the letters, spanning the entire history of the United States. Though Washington directed his address to a small community of Newport Jews, it was understood, from the beginning, that his words carried far wider significance. In defining religious liberty as an "inherent natural right" and promising that "the Government of the United States. . . gives to bigotry no sanction, to persecution no assistance," George Washington set a high bar, not only for his successors, but for Americans of every faith and creed.

The American Star (George Washington)
Frederick Kemmelmeyer, ca. 1803
Gift of Edgar William and Bernice Chrysler Garbisch, 1962 (62.256.7).
The Metropolitan Museum of Art, New York, NY, U.S.A.
Image copyright: The Metropolitan Museum of Art. Image source: Art Resource, NY

To the President of the United States of America.

Sir

Permit the children of the stock of Abraham[1]
to approach you with the most cordial affection and esteem for
your person and merits — and to join with our fellow citizens[2]
in welcoming you to NewPort.

With pleasure we reflect on those days — those days of difficulty,
and danger, when the God of Israel, who delivered David
from the peril of the sword,[3] — shielded Your head
in the day of battle: — and we rejoice to think, that the same
Spirit, who rested in the Bosom of the greatly beloved Daniel[4]
enabling him to preside over the Provinces of the Babylonish
Empire, rests and ever will rest upon you, enabling you to
discharge the arduous duties of Chief Magistrate[5] in these
States.

Deprived as we heretofore have been of the invaluable
rights of free Citizens,[6] we now with a deep sense

[1] In colonial America, the word "Jew" carried negative associations in some Christian circles. Therefore, in writing to George Washington, Newport's Jews used a more positive term which, ironically, they found in the King James version of the Book of Acts (13:26) which describes Paul's address to "Men and brethren, children of the stock of Abraham."

[2] In 1790, Jews could speak of themselves as "fellow citizens" almost nowhere else in the world. Newport's Jews emphasized this point in the opening sentence of their address. Later in the text, they again underscored how much citizenship meant to them: "Deprived as we heretofore have been of the invaluable rights of free Citizens…".

[3] From Psalms 144:10, this verse is also included in the traditional Jewish prayer for the government (hanoten teshu'a), regularly recited in early American synagogues.

[4] Daniel 5-6. Note that Babylon, where Daniel resided, was, like America, a diaspora land. The various references to Daniel, an apocalyptic book of the Bible, also hint at an apocalyptic interpretation of the American Revolution. Some Jews viewed the colonists' miraculous victory as a harbinger of the messiah.

[5] The term "president" had not yet come into common usage.

[6] In 1762, Aaron Lopez and Isaac Elizer had petitioned to obtain naturalization in Newport, and were denied. The court ruled that the 1740 Naturalization Act only applied to under-populated settlements and that local law limited citizenship to believing Christians. This may well have been what Newport's Jews had in mind when writing to the President.

of gratitude to the Almighty disposer[7] of all events behold a Government, erected by the Majesty of the People. — a Government, which to bigotry gives no sanction, to persecution no assistance— but generously affording to all Liberty of conscience, and immunities of Citizenship[8] : — deeming every one, of whatever Nation, tongue, or language equal parts of the great governmental Machine: — This so ample and extensive Federal Union whose basis is Philanthropy, Mutual confidence and Public Virtue, we cannot but acknowledge to be the work of the Great God, who ruleth in the Armies of Heaven and among the Inhabitants of the Earth,[9] doing whatever seemeth him good.

For all these Blessings of civil and religious liberty which we enjoy under an equal and benign administration, we desire to send up our thanks to the Ancient of Days,[10] the great preserver of Men[11]— beseeching him, that the Angel who conducted our forefathers through the wilderness[12] into the promised Land, may graciously conduct you through all the difficulties and dangers of this mortal life: — And, when, like Joshua[13] full of days and full of honour, you are gathered to your Fathers, may you be admitted into the Heavenly Paradise to partake of the water of life, and the tree of immortality.[14]

Done and Signed by order of the Hebrew Congregation[15] in NewPort, Rhode Island August 17, 1790

Moses Seixas,[16] Warden

7   On March 20, 1779, the Continental Congress employed a similar term: "WHEREAS, in just Punishment of our manifold Transgressions it hath pleased the Supreme Disposer of all Events to visit these United States with a calamitous War…".

8   Washington understood that the Jewish community sought his personal guarantee that Jews would be included in the word "all." He therefore sent the congregation's words back to them as if they were his own: "All possess alike liberty of conscience and immunities of citizenship." His slight modification of language is nevertheless noteworthy. The Jewish community viewed its liberty as an act of American generosity ("generously affording"). George Washington let Jews know that they possessed these liberties and immunities as a matter of right ("all possess alike").

9   Daniel 4:32 (4:35 in King James Version).

10   Daniel 7:9.

11   Job 7:20.

12   Exodus 23:20.

13   The comparison to the biblical Joshua was apt for he both entered the Promised Land and, like Washington, was a military leader.

14   Judaism does not hold that heaven is restricted only to Jews. Here Washington is considered to be among "the righteous among the nations" who will find their repose in paradise.

15   Once again, the congregation deliberately avoided using the term "Jewish" (see n. 1). The official name of the "Hebrew Congregation" was Yeshuat Israel (Salvation of Israel), and it became known as the Touro Synagogue in the nineteenth century.

16   Moses Mendes Seixas (1744–1809) of Newport signed the letter to Washington in the name of the city's entire Jewish community. Seixas was a banker, an organizer of the Bank of Rhode Island, the grand master of Rhode Island's Masons, and a Jewish communal leader. He was also a community leader and served as both *parnas* (president or, as he was sometimes called, "warden") of Newport's Jewish congregation. His brother was Gershom Seixas, famed *hazan* (reader) of Congregation Shearith Israel in New York.

To the Hebrew Congregation in Newport Rhode Island

Gentlemen,

While I receive, with much satisfaction, your Address replete with expressions of affection and esteem; I rejoice in the opportunity of assuring you, that I shall always retain a grateful remembrance of the cordial welcome I experienced in my visit to Newport,[1] from all classes of Citizens.[2]

The reflection on the days of difficulty and danger which are past is rendered the more sweet, from a consciousness that they are succeeded by days of uncommon prosperity and security. If we have wisdom to make the best use of the advantages with which we are now favored, we cannot fail, under the just administration of a good Government, to become a great and a happy people.[3]

The Citizens of the United States of America have a right to applaud themselves for having given to mankind examples of an enlarged and liberal policy: a policy worthy of imitation.[4]

[1] The use of the past tense confirms that Washington did not send his letter from Newport, but after he had departed. The letter to the Jews of Newport is undated, but since the handwriting is that of Tobias Lear, who did not accompany Washington to Newport, there can be no doubt that it was sent from New York.

[2] Just as the Jews referred to themselves as "citizens" in the first sentence of their letter, so Washington underscored in his first sentence that they form a "class of citizens".

[3] Washington wrote in a similar vein to other groups. See, for example, his letter to Roman Catholics in America (March 1790): "The prospect of national prosperity now before us is truly animating, and ought to excite the exertions of all good men to establish and secure the happiness of their Country, in the permanent duration of its Freedom and Independence. America, under the smiles of a Divine Providence—the protection of a good Government—and the cultivation of manners, morals and piety, cannot fail of attaining an uncommon degree of eminence, in literature, commerce, agriculture, improvements at home and respectability abroad." A transcript of this letter is printed later in this catalogue.

[4] The idea that America would serve as an example to other countries was commonplace at that time. The bishops of the Methodist Episcopal Church, for example, praised the Constitution in a letter to Washington as "at present the admiration of the world, and may in future become its great exemplar for imitation." Washington himself had used similar language in his letter to the Hebrew Congregation of Savannah: "Happily the people of the United States of America have, in many instances, exhibited examples worthy of imitation."

All possess alike liberty of conscience and immunities of citizenship. It is now no more that toleration is spoken of,[5] as if it was by the indulgence of one class of people, that another enjoyed the exercise of their inherent natural rights.[6] For happily the Government of the United States, which gives to bigotry no sanction, to persecution no assistance,[7] requires only that they who live under its protection should demean themselves as good citizens,[8] in giving it on all occasions their effectual support.

It would be inconsistent with the frankness of my character not to avow that I am pleased with your favorable opinion of my Administration, and fervent wishes for my felicity. May the Children of the Stock of Abraham, who dwell in this land, continue to merit and enjoy the good will of the other Inhabitants; while every one shall sit in safety under his own vine and fig-tree,[9] and there shall be none to make him afraid. May the father of all mercies scatter light and not darkness in our paths, and make us all in our several vocations useful here, and in his own due time and way everlastingly happy.[10]

G. Washington

5 Washington's aside concerning toleration has long puzzled scholars, for the Jewish community made no mention of toleration in their letter to him. Moreover, the indulgent religious "toleration" practiced by the British and much of enlightened Europe was generally viewed with favor by Jews, especially when contrasted to the intolerant treatment and second-class legal status that plagued them elsewhere in the world. The idea that toleration was inadequate, implying less than complete religious freedom, is more closely associated with Thomas Jefferson than with George Washington. For this reason, the editor of Jefferson's papers suggested that Jefferson himself added these words to the letter. Yet in 1789, in corresponding with Quakers, Washington also had made clear that liberty of worship belonged to the category of "rights" and not just of "toleration."

6 The language of "inherent natural rights" distinguished religious liberty in the United States from Jewish "emancipation" in Europe. In Europe, emancipation was generally a "quid pro quo" arrangement. It assumed that Jews would change their ways and left open the possibility (often later realized) that privileges granted to Jews would be taken away if they did not sufficiently "improve." Washington, by contrast, described religious liberty as an "inherent natural right" that can never be taken away.

7 This phrase became the most frequently quoted passage from the letter. It improved upon a phrase used by Newport's Jews in their letter to the President.

8 Some scholars argue that Washington's use of the phrase "demean themselves as good citizens" actually conditioned his promise of religious liberty, as if it only held as long as Jews maintained appropriate behavior. Others point to the fact that Washington frequently linked discussions of liberty with the need for Americans to "demean themselves as good citizens." In the wake of widespread resistance to federal taxation, as evidenced by Shays' Rebellion (1786-87) in Massachusetts and the Whiskey Rebellion (1790s) in Western Pennsylvania, his concern for responsible citizenship is perhaps unsurprising. In his letter to the United Baptist Churches of Virginia (May 1789), he made clear that he held people of every faith to the same standard of good citizenship: "I have often expressed my sentiment, that every man, conducting himself as a good citizen, and being accountable to God alone for his religious opinions, ought to be protected in worshipping the Deity according to the dictates of his own conscience." A transcript of this letter is printed later in this catalogue.

9 A close study of this phrase revealed that this particular biblical passage, that of the ancient Hebrew blessing and prophetic vision of the New Jerusalem in which every man sits safely "under his vine and under his fig tree," was employed by Washington in his own writings more than any other passage. Like the Puritans, he evokes the idea of Zion being in America, as if the prophet's vision would find its fulfillment in the United States. That he applied his own favorite scriptural phrase to the Jewish people is extraordinary.

10 The Declaration of Independence had declared "life, liberty and the pursuit of happiness" to be "unalienable rights." Happiness, at that time, implied not just an emotional state, but a deeper sense of wellbeing.

Bibliography

Boyd, Julian P., ed. *The Papers of Thomas Jefferson*. Vol. 19. Princeton, NJ: Princeton University Press, 1974. 610n.8.

"Congressional Prayer Proclamation, 1779."
    http://www.beliefnet.com/resourcelib/docs/35/Congressional_Prayer_Proclamation_1779_1.html
    (accessed 23 May 2012).

Crackel, Theodore J., ed. *The Papers of George Washington Digital Edition*. Charlottesville: University of Virginia Press,
    Rotunda, 2008; http://rotunda.upress.virginia.edu/founders/ (accessed 01 Jun 2012).

Diner, Hasia R. *The Jews of the United States, 1654 to 2000*. Berkeley: University of California, 2004.

Dreisbach, Daniel L. "The 'Vine and Fig Tree' in George Washington's Letters: Reflections on a Biblical Motif in the Literature
    of the American Founding Era." *Anglican and Episcopal History 76*, no. 3 (September 2007): 299.

Hirschfeld, Fritz. *George Washington and the Jews*. Newark: University of Delaware Press, 2005.

Kammen, Michael. *A Machine That Would Go of Itself: The Constitution in American Culture*. New York: Knopf, 1986.

Kramer, Michael P. "Biblical Typology and the Jewish American Imagination." In *The Turn Around Religion in America:
    Literature, Culture, and the Work of Sacvan Bercovitch*. Edited by Nan Goodman and Michael P. Kramer. Burlington, VT:
    Ashgate, 2011.

Marcus, Jacob R. *The Colonial American Jew, 1492–1776*. Vol. 3. Detroit: Wayne State University Press, 1970.

Osgood, Samuel. *Remarks on the Book of Daniel and on the Revelations*. New York: Greenleaf's Press, 1794.

Sarna, Jonathan D., and David G. Dalin. *Religion and State in the American Jewish Experience*. Notre Dame, IN: University of
    Notre Dame Press, 1997.

Exhibition Checklist

*transcript/translation provided

1 *A Bill for Establishing Religious Freedom, Printed for the Consideration of the People*
Drafted by Thomas Jefferson
Williamsburg?, Virginia, ca. 1779
Courtesy of the Trustees of the Boston Public Library/Rare Books

2 *Declaration of Independence*
Salem, Massachusetts: Ezekiel Russell (or John Rogers at Russell's printing office), ca. July 13-15, 1776
Anonymous. Courtesy of Seth Kaller, Inc

3 Letter from Jonas Phillips to the federal convention, September 7, 1787*
National Archives, Washington, DC

4 The United States Constitution
The Pennsylvania Packet
Philadelphia, Pennsylvania: John Dunlap and David Claypoole, September 19, 1787
Courtesy of David Rubenstein

5 Prayer for the country, Richmond, Virginia, 1789*
National Museum of American Jewish History, 1979.10.1b, a gift from ARA Services, Inc.
Conservation funds provided by the Robert Saligman Charitable Fund

6 Ratification of the Bill of Rights by the Commonwealth of Pennsylvania, 1790
National Archives, Washington, DC

7 Portrait of George Washington (The Dunn-Robinson Portrait of Washington)
Gilbert Charles Stuart (1755-1828), ca. 1800
Philadelphia Museum of Art
Gift of the Honorable Walter H. Annenberg and Leonore Annenberg and the Annenberg Foundation, 2007

8 Commemorative button, ca. 1789-99
Courtesy of the Mount Vernon Ladies' Association, Purchased by the A. Alfred Taubman Fund, 2005

1

8

9

16 Letter to George Washington from the Hebrew Congregation of the City of Savannah*
The Providence Gazette and Country Journal, July 3, 1790
National Museum of American Jewish History, 1986.18.1

17 Letter to George Washington from the Hebrew Congregations in Philadelphia, New York, Charleston, and Richmond, December 13, 1790*
Collection of Congregation Mikveh Israel, Philadelphia

18 Letter from George Washington to the Hebrew Congregations in Philadelphia, New York, Charleston, and Richmond, 1790*
Collection of Congregation Mikveh Israel, Philadelphia

19 Manuel Josephson
Attributed to Lawrence Kilburn (1720–1775)
Arnold and Deanne Kaplan Collection of Early American Judaica

20 Rachel Josephson (wife of Manuel Josephson)
Attributed to Lawrence Kilburn (1720–1775)
Arnold and Deanne Kaplan Collection of Early American Judaica

21 Letter from Thomas Jefferson to Mordecai Manuel Noah, May 28, 1818
Collection of Yeshiva University Museum, Gift of Erica and Ludwig Jesselson

22 Bonbonnière, ca. 1801, decorated with Thomas Jefferson's inaugural address
Collection of Congregation Mikveh Israel, Philadelphia

21

29

Transcripts of Selected Documents

Jonas Phillips to the President and Members of the Constitutional Convention, September 7, 1787

Sires,

With leave and submission I address myself To those in whom there is wisdom understanding and knowledge, they are the honourable personages appointed and Made overseers of a part of the terrestrial globe of the Earth, Namely the 13 united states of america in Convention Assembled, the Lord preserve them amen—

I the subscriber being one of the people called Jews of the City of Philadelphia, a people scattered and dispersed among all nations do behold with Concern that among the Laws in the Constitution of Pennsylvania, there is a Clause Sect 10 to viz—I do believe in one God the Creatur and governor of the universe and the Rewarder of the good and the punisher of the wicked—and I do acknowledge the Scriptures of the old and New testament to be given by a divine inspiration—to swear and believe that the new testament was given by divine inspiration is absolutely against the Religious principle of a Jew, and is against his Conscience to take any such oath—By the above law a Jew is deprived of holding any publick office or place of Government which is a Contridictory to the bill of Right Sect 2 viz

That all men have a natural and unalienable Right to worship almighty God according to the dictates of their own Conscience and understanding and that no man ought or of Right can be Compelled to attend any Religious Worship or Creed or support any place of worship or Maintain any minister contrary to or against his own free will and Consent, nor can any man who acknowledges the being of a God be Justly deprived or abridged of any Civil Right as a Citizen on account of his Religious sentiments or peculiar mode of Religious Worship, and that no authority can or ought to be vested in or assumed by any power whatever that shall in any case interfere or in any manner Controul the Right of Conscience in the free Exercise of Religious Worship,—

It is well known among all the Citizens of the 13 united states that the Jews have been true and faithful whigs, and during the late Contest with England they have been foremost in aiding and assisting the states with their lifes and fortunes, they have supported the cause, have bravely fought and bled for liberty which they can not Enjoy—

Therefore if the honourable Convention shall in their Wisdom think fit and alter the said oath and leave out the words to viz—and I do acknowledge the scripture of the new testament to be given by divine inspiration, then the Israelites will think themself happy to live under a government where all Religious societys are on an Equal footing—I solicit this favour for myself my children and posterity and for the benefit of all the Israelites through the 13 united states of America.

My prayers is unto the Lord. May the people of this states Rise up as a great and young lion, May they prevail against their Enemies, may the degrees of honour of his Excellencey the president of the Convention George Washington, be Exhalted and Raise up. May Everyone speak of his glorious Exploits.

May God prolong his days among us in this land of Liberty—May he lead the armies against his Enemys as he has done hereuntofore—May God Extend peace unto the united states—May they get up to the highest Prosperitys—May God Extend peace to them and their seed after them so long as the Sun and moon Endureth— and May the almighty God of our father Abraham Isaac and Jacob indue this Noble Assembly with wisdom Judgment and unanimity in their Counsells and may they have the satisfaction to see that their present toil and labour for the wellfair of the united states may be approved of Through all the world and particular by the united, states of America, is the ardent prayer of Sires

Your most devoted obed. Servant

Jonas Phillips

Philadelphia 24th *Ellul* 5547 or Sepr 7th 1787

English Translation

Hear us when we call O God of Righteousness
Thous hast enlarged us when in distress, have mercy upon us and hear our prayers--
Thou O Lord! did deliver us from our Strong Ennemy and from them that hated us for
they were to [sic] strong for us--
For Thou Girded us with strength to the Battle thou hast subdued
those that rose up against us
And Thou O Lord did send us a Deliverer in the Head of this Nation the President of
the United States
Therefore we humbly supplicate Thee O Lord, to give him an understanding Heart,
to Govern the People, cause us to rejoice in his days, that he may live and not see
Corruption, that he may discern between Good and Evil, and we beseech Thee o Lord,
to conduct him in a perfect way, that his administration may be long and prosperous
and the Nation happy, We beseech Thee O Lord to have the U.S. Senators and
Representatives of the U.S. and all the Rulers of the Land under Thy Holy Protection,
Grant them such a share of knowledge as will tend to the happiness of the people, and
the advancement of thy Glory, that they may wisely and successfully execute the Trust
Committed to their Care, that knowledge, Religion and Piety, Arts and Sciences, may
increase, and that Agriculture and Manufactures, Trade and commerce, may flourish
That thou wilt Save them and us from the hands of Strange Nations, that our Sons may
be a[s] Plants grownup, in their Youth, that our Daughters may be as Corner Stones,
that our Granarys may be full affording all manner of store, that our Sheep may bring
forth
Thousands of tens of Thousands in our Streets, that our Oxen may be strong to labour,
that there be no complaining in these States, may the people and their Rulers be
happy and Glory in The Lord, May Judah be saved and Israel dwell in Safety, which
god in his infinite mercy grant, and let us say Amen.

To the Ministers, Church Wardens and Vestrymen of the German Lutheran Congregation
in and near Philadelphia

Gentlemen,

  While I request you to accept my thanks for your kind address, I must profess
myself highly gratified by the sentiments of esteem and consideration contained in it.
The approbation my past conduct has received from so worthy a body of citizens as
that, whose joy for my appointment you announce, is a proof of the indulgence with
which my future transactions will be judged by them.

  I could not however avoid apprehending that the partiality of my Countrymen
in favor of the measures now pursued has led them to expect too much from the
present Government; did not the same Providence, which has been visible in every
stage of our progress to this interesting crisis, from a combination of circumstances,
give us cause to hope for the accomplishment of all our reasonable desires.

  Thus partaking with you in the pleasing anticipation of the blessings of a wise
and efficient government; I flatter myself that opportunities will not be wanting for
me to show my disposition to encourage the domestic and public virtues of Industry,
Economy, Patriotism, Philanthropy, and that Righteousness which exalteth a Nation.

  I rejoice in having so suitable an occasion to testify the reciprocity of my
esteem for the numerous People whom you represent. From the excellent character
for diligence, sobriety and virtue, which the Germans in general, who are settled
in America, have ever maintained; I cannot forbear felicitating myself on receiving
from so respectable a number of them such strong assurances of their affection, for
my person, confidence in my integrity, and zeal to support me in my endeavours for
promoting the welfare of our common Country.

  So long as my Conduct shall merit the approbation of the <u>Wise</u> and the <u>Good</u>,
I hope to hold the same place in your affections, which your friendly declarations
induce me to believe I possess at present: and, amidst all the vicissitudes that may
await me in this mutable existence, I shall earnestly desire the continuation of an
interest in your intercessions at the <u>Throne</u> of <u>Grace.</u>

G. Washington

To the General Committee representing the United Baptist Churches in Virginia

Gentlemen,

I request that you will accept my best acknowledgements for your congratulation on my appointment to the first office in the nation. The kind manner in which you mention my past conduct equally claims the expression of my gratitude.

After we had, by the smiles of Heaven on our exertions, obtained the object for which we contended, I retired at the conclusion of the war, with an idea that my country would have no farther occasion for my services, and with the intention of never entering again into public life. But when the exigence of my country seemed to require me once more to engage in public affairs, an honest conviction of duty superseded my former resolution, and became my apology for deviating from the happy plan which I had adopted.

If I could have entertained the slightest apprehension that the Constitution framed in the Convention, where I had the honor to preside, might possibly endanger the religious rights of any ecclesiastical society, certainly I would never have placed my signature to it; and if I could now conceive that the general Government might ever be so administered as to render the liberty of conscience insecure, I beg you will be persuaded that no one would be more zealous than myself to establish effectual barriers against the horrors of spiritual tyranny, and every species of religious persecution.—For you, doubtless, remember that I have often expressed my sentiment, that every man, conducting himself as a good citizen, and being accountable to God alone for his religious opinions, ought to be protected in worshipping the Deity according to the dictates of his own conscience.

While I recollect with satisfaction that the religious society of which you are members, have been, throughout America, uniformly, and almost unanimously, the firm friends to civil liberty, and the persevering Promoters of our glorious revolution; I cannot hesitate to believe that they will be the faithful supporters of a free, yet efficient general Government. Under this pleasing expectation I rejoice to assure them that they may rely on my best wishes and endeavors to advance their prosperity.

In the meantime be assured, Gentlemen, that I entertain a proper sense of your fervent supplications to God for my temporal and eternal happiness.

G. Washington

To the President of the United States.

Sir,

WE the bishops of the Methodist-Episcopal church, humbly beg leave, in the name of our society collectively in these United States, to express to you the warm feelings of our hearts, and our sincere congratulations, on your appointment to the Presidentship of these States. We are conscious from the signal proofs you have already given, that you are a friend of mankind; and under this established idea, place as a full a confidence in your wisdom and integrity, for the preservation of those civil and religious liberties which have been transmitted to us by the providence of GOD, and the glorious revolution, as we believe, out to be reposed in man.

We have received the most grateful satisfaction, from the humble and entire dependance on the great Governor of the universe which you have repeatedly expressed, acknowledging him the source of every blessing, and particularly of the most excellent constitution of these States, which is at present the admiration of the world, and may in future become its great exemplar of imitation and hence we enjoy a holy expectation that you will always prove a faithful and impartial Patron of genuine, vital religion – the grand end of our creation and present probationary existence. And we promise you our fervent prayers to the throne of grace, that GOD Almighty may endue you with all the graces and gifts of his Holy Spirit, that may enable you to fill up your important station to his glory, the good of his church, the happiness and prosperity of the United States, and the welfare of mankind.

Signed in behalf of the Methodist-Episcopal Church,
Thomas Coke
Francis Asbury
New-York, May 19, 1789.

To The Bishops of the Methodist-Episcopal church in the United States of *America*.

Gentlemen,

      I return to you individually, and (through you) to your society collectively in the United States, my thanks for the demonstration of affection, and the expressions of joy offered in their behalf, on my late appointment. It shall still be my endeavor to manifest by overt acts, the purity of my inclinations for promoting the happiness of mankind; as well as the sincerity of my desires to contribute whatever may be in my power towards the preservation of the civil and religious liberties of the American people. In pursuing this line of conduct, I hope by the assistance of divine providence, not altogether to disappoint the confidence which you have been pleased to repose in me.

      It always affords me satisfaction when I find a concurrence in sentiment and practice between all conscientious men, in acknowledgments of homage to the Great Governor of the Universe, and in professions of support to a just civil government. After mentioning that I trust the people of every denomination, who demean themselves as good citizens, will have occasion to be convinced, that I shall always strive to prove a faithful and impartial Patron of genuine, vital religion; I must allure you in particular that I take in the kindest part the promise you make of presenting your prayers at the throne of grace for me, and that I likewise implore the Divine benedictions on yourselves and your religious community.

G. Washington

To the President of the United States.

      The Address of the Religious Society called Quakers, from their yearly Meeting for Pennsylvania, New Jersey, Delaware, and the western parts of Virginia and Maryland

      Being met in this our annual Assembly, for the well ordering the Affairs of our religious Society, and the Promotion of universal Righteousness, our Minds have been drawn to consider that the Almighty, who ruleth in Heaven, and in the Kingdoms of Men, having permitted a great Revolution to take place in the Government of this Country, we are fervently concerned that the Rulers of the People may be favoured with the Counsel of God; the only sure means of enabling them to fulfill the important Trust committed to their charge; and in an especial manner, that Divine Wisdom and Grace vouchsafed from above, may qualify thee, to fill up the Duties of the exalted station to which thou art appointed.

      We are sensible thou hast obtained great place in the Esteem and Affection of People of all Denominations, over whom thou presideth, and many eminent Talents being committed to thy Trust, we much desire they may be fully devoted to the Lord's Honor and Service, that thus thou mayest be an happy Instrument in his Hand, for the Suppression of Vice, Infidelity, and Irreligion, and every species of Oppression on the Persons or Consciences of Men, so that Righteousness and Peace, which truly exalt a nation, may prevail throughout the Land, as the only solid Foundation that can be laid for Prosperity and Happiness of this or any Country.

      The free Toleration which the Citizens of these States enjoy in the public Worship of the Almighty agreeable to the Dictates of their Consciences, we esteem among the choicest of Blessings, and we desire to be filled with fervent Charity for those who differ from us in matters of Faith and Practice, believing that the general Assembly of Saints is composed of the sincere and upright hearted of all Nations, Kingdoms, and People, so we trust we may justly claim it from others, and in a full persuasion that the Divine Principle we profess, leads into Harmony and Concord, we can take no part in carrying on War on any Occasion or under any Power, but are bound in Conscience to lead quiet and peaceable Lives, in Godliness and Honesty among Men, contributing, freely, our Proportion to the Indigencies of the poor, and to the necessary Support of civil Government, acknowledging those who rule well to be worthy of double honor, and if any professing with us, are, or have been of a contrary Disposition and Conduct, we own them not herein, having never been chargeable from our first establishment as a religious Society, with fomenting or countenancing Tumults or Conspiracies, or Disrespect to those who are placed in Authority over us.

We wish not improperly to intrude on thy Time or Patience, nor is it our Practice to offer Adulation to any, but as we are a People whose Principles and Conduct have been misrepresented and traduced, we take the Liberty to assure thee, that we feel our Hearts affectionately drawn towards thee, and those in Authority over us, with Prayers that thy Presidency may, under the Blessing of Heaven, be happy to thyself and to the People, that thru the increase of Morality and true Religion, Divine Providence may condescend to look down upon our Land with a propitious Eye, and bless the Inhabitants with the Continuance of Peace, the Dew of Heaven, and the Fatness of the Earth, and enable us gratefully to acknowledge His manifold Mercies, and it is our earnest concern that he may be pleased to grant thee every necessary Qualification to fill thy weighty and important Station to his Glory, so that finally, when all Terrestrial Honors shall fail and pass away, thou, and thy respectable Consort may be found worthy to receive a Crown of unfading Righteousness, in the Mansions of Peace and Joy forever.

Signed in and on behalf of Meeting held in Philadelphia
Nicholas Wain
Clerk to the meeting this year

To the Religious Society called Quakers, at their Yearly Meeting for Pennsylvania, New Jersey, Delaware, and the Western Part of Maryland and Virginia.

I receive with pleasure your affectionate address, and thank you for the friendly sentiments and good wishes, which you express for the success of my administration and for my personal happiness.—

We have reason to rejoice in the prospect that the present National Government, which by the favor of Divine Providence, was formed by the common Counsels, and peaceably established with the common consent of the People, will prove a blessing to every denomination of them. –To render it such, my best endeavors shall not be wanting.

Government being, among other purposes, instituted to protect the Persons and Consciences of men from oppression, it certainly is the duty of Rulers, not only to abstain from it themselves, but according to their stations, to prevent it in others.—

The liberty enjoyed by the people of these States, of worshipping Almighty God agreeable to their consciences, is not only among the choicest of their Blessings, but also of their Rights.—While men perform their social Duties faithfully, they do all that Society or the State can with propriety demand or expect; and remain responsible only to their Maker for the Religion, or modes of faith, which they may prefer or profess.

Your principles and conduct are well known to me—and it is doing the People called Quakers no more than Justice to say, that (except their declining to share with others the burden of the common defence) there is no denomination among us who are more exemplary and useful citizens.—

I assure you very explicitly that in my opinion the Conscientious scruples of all men should be treated with great delicacy and tenderness, and it is my wish and desire that the laws may always be as extensively accommodated to them, as a due regard to the Protection and essential interests of the nation may justify and permit.—

G. Washington

To the Roman Catholics in the United States of America.

Gentlemen,

While I now receive with much satisfaction your congratulations on my being called, by an unanimous vote, to the first station in my Country; I cannot but duly notice your politeness in offering an apology for the unavoidable delay. As that delay has given you an opportunity of realizing, instead of anticipating, the benefits of the general Government; you will do me the justice to believe, that your testimony of the increase of the public prosperity, enhances the pleasure which I should otherwise have experienced from your affectionate address.

I feel that my conduct, in war and in peace, has met with more general approbation than could reasonably have been expected: and I find myself disposed to consider that fortunate circumstance, in a great degree, resulting from the able support and extraordinary candour of my fellow-citizens of all denominations.

The prospect of national prosperity now before us is truly animating, and ought to excite the exertions of all good men to establish and secure the happiness of their Country, in the permanent duration of its Freedom and Independence. America, under the smiles of a Divine Providence—the protection of a good Government—and the cultivation of manners, morals and piety, cannot fail of attaining an uncommon degree of eminence, in literature, commerce, agriculture, improvements at home and respectability abroad.

As mankind become more liberal they will be more apt to allow, that all those who conduct themselves as worthy members of the Community are equally entitled to the protection of civil Government. I hope ever to see America among the foremost nations in examples of justice and liberality. And I presume that your fellow-citizens will not forget the patriotic part which you took in the accomplishment of their Revolution, and the establishment of their Government: or the important assistance which they received from a nation in which the Roman Catholic faith is professed.

I thank you, Gentlemen, for your kind concern for me. While my life and my health shall continue, in whatever situation I may be, it shall be my constant endeavour to justify the favourable sentiments which you are pleased to express of my conduct. And may the members of your Society in America, animated alone by the pure spirit of Christianity, and still conducting themselves as the faithful subjects of our free Government, enjoy every temporal and spiritual felicity.

G. Washington

Sir,

We have long been anxious of congratulating you on your appointment, by unanimous approbation, to the Presidential dignity of this country and of testifying our unbounded confidence in your integrity and unblemished virtue; yet, however exalted the station you now fill, it is still not equal to the merit of your heroic services through an arduous and dangerous conflict which has embosomed you in the hearts of her citizens.

Our eccentric situation added to a diffidence founded on the most profound respect has thus long prevented our address; yet the delay has realized anticipation, given us an opportunity of presenting our grateful acknowledgments for the benediction of Heaven through the energy of federal influence, and the equity of your administration.

Your unexampled liberality and extensive philanthropy have dispelled that cloud of bigotry and superstition which has long, as a veil, shaded religion—unriveted the fetters of enthusiasm—enfranchised us with all the privileges and immunities of free citizens, and initiated us into the grand mass of legislative mechanism. By example you have taught us to endure the ravages of war with manly fortitude, and to enjoy the blessings of peace with reverence to the Deity and with benignity and love to our fellow creatures.

May the Great Author of worlds grant you all happiness- an uninterrupted series of health—addition of years to the number of your days, and a continuance of guardianship to that freedom, which, under auspices of Heaven, your magnanimity and wisdom have given these States.

Levi Sheftal, President.
In behalf of the Hebrew Congregation

Gentlemen,

I thank you with great sincerity for your congratulations on my appointment to the office, which I have the honor to hold by the unanimous choice of my fellow-citizen; and especially for the expressions which you are pleased to use in testifying the confidence that is reposed in me by your congregation.

As the delay which has naturally intervened between my election and your address has afforded me an opportunity for appreciating the merits of the federal government and for communicating your sentiments of its administration—I have rather to express my satisfaction rather than regret at a circumstance, which demonstrates, upon experiment, your attachment to the former as well as approbation of the latter.

I rejoice that a spirit of liberality and philanthropy is much more prevalent than it formerly was among the enlightened nations of the earth; and that your brethren will benefit thereby in proportion as it shall become still more extensive. Happily the people of the United States have, in many instances, exhibited examples worthy of imitation: The salutary influence of which will doubtless extend much farther, if, gratefully enjoying those blessings of peace which (under the favor of Heaven) have been obtained by fortitude in war, they shall conduct themselves with reverence to the Deity and charity toward their fellow-creatures.

May the same wonder-working Deity, who, long since, delivered the Hebrews from their Egyptian oppressors, planted them in a promised land—whose providential agency has lately been conspicuous in establishing these United States as an independent nation—still continue to water them with the dews of Heaven, and to make the inhabitants of every denomination participate in the temporal and spiritual blessings of that people whose God is Jehovah.

G. Washington

The address of the Hebrew Congregations in Philadelphia, New York, Charleston, and Richmond to George Washington

To the President of the United States,

Sir,

It is reserved for you to unite in affection for your Character and Person, every political and religious denomination of Men; and in this will the Hebrew Congregations aforesaid, yield to no class of their fellow Citizens.—

We have been hitherto prevented by various circumstances peculiar to our situation from adding our congratulations to those which the rest of America have offerd on your elevation to the chair of the Federal government. Deign then illustrious Sir, to accept this our homage.—

The wonders which the Lord of Hosts hath worked in the days of our Forefathers, have taught us to observe the greatness of his wisdom and his might—throughout the events of the late glorious revolution: And while we humble ourselves at his footstool in thanksgiving and praise for the blessing of his deliverance; we acknowledge you the Leader of the American Armies as his chosen and beloved servant; But not to your Sword alone is our present happiness to be ascribed; That indeed opend the way to the reign of Freedom, but never was it perfectly secure, till your hand gave birth to the Federal Constitution, and you renounced the joys of retirement to Seal by your administration in Peace, what you had achieved in war.—

To the eternal God who is thy refuge, we commit in our prayer the care of thy precious Life; and when full of years Thou shall be gatherd unto the People, thy righteousness shall go before thee; and we shall remember amidst our regret, that the Lord hath set apart the Godly for himself; whilst thy name and thy Virtues will remain an indelible memorial on our minds.

Manuel Josephson

For and in behalf and under the Authority of the several Congregations aforesaid

Philadelphia 17 Dece 1790

To the Hebrew Congregations in the cities of Philadelphia, New York, Charleston, and Richmond

Gentlemen,

The liberality of sentiment towards each other which marks every political and religious denomination of men in this country, stands unparalleled in the history of Nations.—The affection of such people is a treasure beyond the reach of calculation;—and the repeated proofs which my fellow Citizens have given of their attachment to me, and approbation of my doings form the purest source of my temporal felicity.—The affectionate expressions of your address again excite my gratitude, and receive my warmest acknowledgment.—

The Power and Goodness of the Almighty were strongly manifested in the events of our late glorious revolution; and his kind interposition in our behalf has been no less visible in the establishment of our present equal government.—In war he directed the Sword; and in peace he has ruled in our Councils.—My agency in both has been guided by the best intentions, and a sense of the duty which I owe my Country:—and as my exertions have hitherto been amply rewarded by the Approbation of my fellow Citizens, I shall endeavour to deserve a continuance of it by my future conduct.

May the same temporal and eternal blessings which you implore for me, rest upon your Congregations.

G. Washington

Monticello May 28. 18.

Sir,

I thank you for the Discourse on the consecration of the Synagogue in your city, with which you have been pleased to favor me. I have read it with pleasure and instruction, having learnt from it some valuable facts in Jewish history which I did not know before. Your sect, by its sufferings, has furnished a remarkable proof of the universal spirit of religious intolerance inherent in every sect, disclaimed by all while feeble, and practiced by all when in power. Our laws have applied the only antidote to this vice, protecting our religious as they do our civil rights, by putting all on an equal footing. But more remains to be done, for altho' we are free by the law, we are not so in practice; public opinion erects itself into an Inquisition, and exercises its office with as much fanaticism as fans the flames of an Auto da fé. The prejudice still scowling on your section of our religion, altho' the elder one, cannot be unfelt by yourselves; it is to be hoped that individual dispositions will at length mould themselves to the model of the law and consider the moral basis on which all our religions rest, as a rallying point which unites them in a common interest; while the peculiar dogmas branching from it are the exclusive concern of the respective sects embracing them, and no rightful subject of notice to any other; public opinion needs reformation on this point, which would have the further happy effect of doing away the hypocritical maxim of 'Intus ut lubet, foris ut moris. [with as pleases, without how maintained]' Nothing, I think, would be so likely to effect this, as to your sect particularly as the more careful attention to education, which you recommend, and which, placing its members on the equal and commanding benches of science, will exhibit them as equal objects of respect and favor. I should not do full justice to the merits of your discourse, were I not in addition to that of its matter, to express my consideration of it as a fine specimen of style & composition. I salute you with great respect and esteem.

Th. Jefferson

Letters from George Washington to American Religious Communities

April/May 1789 – German Lutherans of Philadelphia

May 1789 – Bishops of the Methodist Episcopal Church, General Assembly of the Presbyterian Church, United Baptist Churches of Virginia

June 1789 – German Reformed Congregations

August 1789 – Moravian Society for Propagating the Gospel, Protestant Episcopal Church

October 1789 – Society of Quakers, Congregational Ministers of New Haven, The Synod of the Dutch Reformed Church in North America

November 1789 – Presbyterian Ministers of Massachusetts and New Hampshire

March 1790 – Society of the Free Quakers, Roman Catholics in America

June 1790 – Hebrew Congregation of Savannah

August 1790 – Hebrew Congregation in Newport, Convention of the Universal Church

December 1790 – Hebrew Congregations in Philadelphia, New York, Charleston, and Richmond

May 1791 – Congregational Church of Midway, Georgia

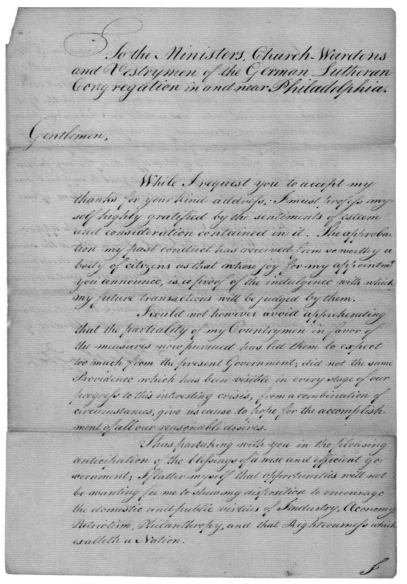

Detail, letter from George Washington to the German Lutheran Congregation in Philadelphia, 1789
Seth Kaller, Inc.

To Bigotry No Sanction: George Washington and Religious Freedom

A Special Exhibition of the National Museum of American Jewish History
June 29 - September 30, 2012

The Museum gratefully acknowledges the Morris Morgenstern Foundation.

This exhibition is made possible by the generous support of the National Museum of American Jewish History Board of Trustees with leadership gifts from: Betsy and Phil Darivoff, Linda and Michael Jesselson, and Roy J. Zuckerberg Family Foundation.

The National Museum of American Jewish History exhibitions and collections staff:
Dr. Josh Perelman, Chief Curator and Director of Exhibitions & Collections
Andrew Beal, Shira Goldstein, Sasha Makuka, Claire Pingel, Ivy Weingram

Exhibition Design: Gallagher & Associates
Exhibition Fabrication: Art Guild, Inc.
Contributing Historian: Dr. Jonathan D. Sarna
Interactive Media: Bluecadet Interactive
Annotated Letters: Courtesy of Facing History and Ourselves and the George Washington Institute for Religious Freedom
Public Relations: Nina Zucker Associates
Catalogue Design: Courtney Ballantine
Copyeditor: Michele Alperin

Special thanks to:
Atelier Art Services
B'nai B'rith International
Boston Public Library Rare Books Department
Congregation Mikveh Israel in Philadelphia
Conservation Center for Art and Historic Artifacts
Haverford College Quaker and Special Collections
Seth Kaller
Deanne and Arnold Kaplan
Mount Vernon Ladies' Association
National Archives
National Constitution Center
Philadelphia Museum of Art
David Rubenstein
Yeshiva University Museum

NATIONAL MUSEUM OF
AMERICAN JEWISH HISTORY